BUILDING UP THE CHURCH

BUILDING UP THE CHURCH

LIVE EXPERIMENTS IN FAITH, HOPE, AND LOVE

SAM EWELL

a study guide for

New Monasticism: What It Has to Say to Today's Church
by Jonathan Wilson-Hartgrove (Brazos, 2008)

WIPF & STOCK · Eugene, Oregon

BUILDING UP THE CHURCH
Live Experiments in Faith, Hope, and Love

Wipf & Stock
A Division of Wipf and Stock Publishers
199 W. 8th Ave., Suite 3
Eugene, OR 97401

www.wipfandstock.com

ISBN 13: 978-1-55635-877-7

Manufactured in the U.S.A.

CONTENTS

PART ONE

SETTING THE STAGE

This is the study guide for School for Conversion's (SFC) 103 course: "Building Up the Church: (Live) Experiments in Faith, Hope, and Love"—the companion volume to Jonathan Wilson-Hartgrove's book, *New Monasticism: What it Has to Say to Today's Church.*[1] As a *study guide* (and not a workbook per se), it is designed as a commentary on the book and as a resource for group study, rather than as a series of ready-made lesson plans to be worked through in a linear way.

This is particularly true of Part 2, which is organized as a collection of resources—stories, reflection questions, suggested exercises—that will be arranged by and adapted for each group of participants. While Part 2 directly engages the "textbook" of the course and functions as the platform for the group session, Part 1 does the work of vision-casting for participation in the course and answers some basic questions in relation to the course and how it fits into the School for Conversion's vision for theological education. So, before you get started with your group sessions, please read Part 1 carefully.

In the introduction to SFC's 101 course: "Introduction to Christianity as a Way of Life," Jonathan Wilson-Hartgrove writes that "new monasticism" has emerged within the fragmentation of contemporary American Christianity "to experiment with new forms of faithfulness"—as an attempt to embody an answer to the question faced by the whole church: "how do we live the gospel of God's kingdom that Jesus taught and practiced at this moment?"

While the 101 course functions as a kind of "movable seminary" that circulates among new monastic communities—both catalyzing and learning from their witness—this course has a different focus. It seeks to catalyze and learn with/from the (local) church about its identity as "God's peculiar people" (Titus 2:14). To do that, we will return to the question mentioned above about the gospel of God's kingdom, sharing some of the results of new monasticism's experiments in order to extend the conversation to the whole church.

So, if we think of this course as an extended conversation, it will be helpful to keep in mind the basic direction of the conversation. Here's a little road map—a sketch of where this conversation is going:

Through the *signs*, *roots*, and *stories* set forth in chapters 2–4 of *New Monasticism*, and through the *practices* elaborated in chapters 5–9, the stage is set for a conversation about how "life together in new monastic communities . . . could be adopted by congregations as a way of living into the story of the people of God." Wilson-Hartgrove continues, "The stories that I tell about what these practices look like in

---

1. Grand Rapids, MI: Brazos, 2008.

communities are not meant as prescriptions for churches, but as catalysts for imagination. My point is not that churches ought to imitate new monastic communities, but that another way is possible."[2]

The book and this course, then—signs, roots, stories, practices and all—are basically about how we participate in God's work of *building up* the church (Eph. 2:22; 4:12; 1 Pet. 2:5). It is an invitation and a summons to carry out *collective experiments in faith, hope, and love.* Keep in mind that these experiments were not designed for heroes; so they do not come with a warning: "Do not try these at home!" In fact, they have been tried and tested by so many quite unheroic people that these experiments actually come with a permission slip: "If you want to know Christ and the power of his resurrection, go ahead and try these. And, yes, these must be tried at home!"

WHAT KIND OF SCHOOL?

It's worth pointing out that School for Conversion is not a "school" in any traditional sense. There are no classrooms, no set curricula, no grades, and no diplomas for those who "pass." (There is homework, however!) In the introduction to the 101 course, Wilson-Hartgrove contrasts the typical "schooling" process with how SFC is trying to do education. Whereas this common understanding of "schooling" tends to focus on transmitting or "passing on" a body of knowledge/information that is not yet known by the student but considered to be essential for successful training, the author casts a quite different vision for education:

> if God really wants to make us into a holy people, it makes sense that we need a *school* for holiness. And if God really wants every part of our lives to be holy, then education in this school will have to cover everything. So this course, like any course, is about learning some stuff you might not have known before. But it's also about how you eat and where you live and what you buy when you go to the store. It's about how you spend your money and who you spend your time with and what you think about when you're walking down the street. This is an introduction to Christianity as a way of life. We believe true education is about *learning to live together the way God made us to live.*[3]

This description echoes something that the late Brazilian educator, Paulo Freire, used to say: "No one educates anyone else" and "No one gets educated alone." His point is that education is really about leading one another to learn from one another. And, if this is the case, a more important question than, What is being taught?, is the question, What are we learning? Or, even better, the question we ought to be asking

2. *New Monasticism,* 70.

3. *School for Conversion 101,* 3.

ourselves constantly is this: How are we *learning to live together the way God made us to live?*

Remember: the goal is not primarily to know more, but rather *to learn from what we are already doing and to know what to do with what we already know.* Getting "schooled" then is the process of learning together how to becomes apprentices of Jesus *in order to* know and live in the truth: "If you continue in my word, you are truly my disciples; and you will know the truth, and the truth will make you free" (John 8:31–32).

CONVERSION AND/AS LEARNING NEW ROLES

Whatever understanding of "conversion" our various church traditions have passed on to us, one thing should remain clear: conversion has to do with the changes that we must undergo as we respond to the grace of Jesus' proclamation: "Repent, for the kingdom of heaven has come near" (Matt. 4:17). This course is part of a School for *Conversion* because we believe that God wants to change us—to shape us by turning us toward the way that leads to life.

In order to fill out what conversion entails, consider the following quote from Brad Kallenberg, which lays out three aspects to conversion:

> First, conversion involves a change in social identity. Second, in large measure, this new social identity is accomplished by the acquisition of new language skills. Finally, conversion is constituted by a paradigm shift that results in bringing the the world into focus in a whole new way. Notice that in all three cases, conversion involves enculturation into community and into a community of a particular sort. The tracks for being a Christ-follower have already been laid by those who faithfully followed him before us. The conceptual language that the new believer learns to speak has been in circulation for two millennia. Moreover, to say that I have shifted paradigms is but an imprecise way of saying that I have changed allegiance from one community to another.[4]

One way to begin to understand how these three aspects of conversion fit together is to think about conversion in the early church. Wilson-Hartgrove describes it this way:

> When the Holy Spirit came on the early church in Antioch, Jews and Gentiles alike trusted Jesus to give them access to God. United in worship, they shared life with one another like a family. No one knew what to make of this at first. They knew what a group of Jews was supposed to be, and they knew what Gentiles looked like, but they weren't sure what to call Jews and Gentiles living

4. Kallenberg, *Live to Tell*, 46.

and worshiping together in Jesus' name. So they decided to make up a new name. They called them 'Christians,' Acts says (11:26).[5]

These three aspects or dynamics of conversion each correspond to a *role* that we need to learn how to play as participants in this course. These three roles are: (1) storytellers, (2) language-learners, and (3) pilgrims.

1) Storyteller

As *storytellers* we have to learn to retell our autobiographies in light of the gospel. Who am I? Who are "my people"? Who's in my family? To whom do we owe ultimate allegiance? We have to go through the same "identity check"—including the "before" and "after" snapshots—given to those at Ephesus (Eph. 2:11–22).

The "before" shot: "remember that at one time you *Gentiles by birth*. . . . remember that you were at that time without Christ, being *aliens*, from the commonwealth of Israel, *strangers* to the covenants of promise, having no hope and *without God* in the world" (Eph. 2:11–12)

The "after" shot: "But now in Christ Jesus, you who once were far off have been brought near by the blood of Christ. . . . So then you are no longer strangers and aliens, but you are *citizens* with the saints and also *members* of the household of God" (Eph. 2:13, 19).

And for us—for whom, regrettably, "'Christian' has become an adjective that we tack on to some more fundamental identity"—to be capable of fully claiming a new social identity, we have to be able to make two key moves as we "play the Bible's game."

First, we have to learn to *read ourselves into the Bible through Christ and find ourselves there*.

Dietrich Bonhoeffer explains it this way:

> It is in fact more important for us to know what God did to Israel, in God's son Jesus Christ, that to discover what God intends for us today. The fact that Jesus Christ died is more important that the fact that I will die. And the fact that Jesus Christ was raised from the dead is the sole ground of my hope that I, too, will be raised on the day of judgment. Our salvation is "from outside ourselves" (*extra nos*). I find salvation not in my life story, but only in the story of Jesus Christ. Only those who allow themselves to be found in Jesus Christ—in the incarnation, the cross, and resurrection—are with God and God with them. . . . What we call our life, our need, our guilt, and our deliverance is by no means the whole of reality; our life, our need, our guilt, and our deliverance are there

---

5. *New Monasticism*, 10.

in the Scriptures. Because it pleased God to act for us there, it is only there that we will be helped. *Only in the Scriptures do we get to know our own story.*[6]

And second, we have to be able to *"read" the world and the "something new" that God is doing there.* So, in becoming good storytellers, we learn to speak of the Bible and history not as two "planes of existences"—that is, "history" as the unfolding of real world events to which we "add on" a biblical gloss. In fact, the kingdom of God and the new creation that the Bible narrates do not refer to another geography from the one we inhabit; they refer to the future of this "world-as-it-is" as it is renewed into the "world-as-it-should-be."

John Calvin taught us to think of the Bible as spectacles through which we look and see the world rightly. It's a great image, because it clearly shows us that while we suffer from blindness, we can *learn* to see. But our talk of reading the world with the Bible or learning to tell a story about the world in light of the biblical story also raises another question that we have to face: how should we read the Bible? How do we learn to use these spectacles?

In answering these questions, it is important to recognize (1) that no one learns to read the Bible by themselves, and (2) that our own sin "dirties the spectacles" in such a way that we need others to help us clean our glasses—or, as Jesus said, to take the log out of our own eye! This course cannot settle all the interpretive questions in advance, but it does offer this "rule of thumb": *let's read the Bible in light of this basic plotline: God's plan is to save the world through a people.*[7]

2) Language Learner

To become tellers of God's story, we also need to become *language learners.* We need to learn to speak a new language about ourselves, the world, and God. And as anyone who has become fluent in a second language will tell you, learning to speak another language goes beyond saying "foreign words." Becoming fluent in another language involves becoming *immersed in another way of life.*

Someone who is fluent in Portuguese can tell you that a *churrasco* is much more than "grilling out"—although that's how a *churrasco* might appear to someone on a visit to Brazil. Likewise, *futebol* may translate into English as the sport we call "soccer," but any Brazilian would tell you that *futebol* is not just a sport, but a quasi-religious phenomenon whose own "liturgical" life comes to a climax every four years with the World Cup!

In the same way, someone who has become fluent in the Christian faith would tell you that *forgiveness* is not just saying "I'm sorry" or "Forget about it." Forgiveness

6. Dietrich Bonhoeffer, *Life Together,* 62; emphasis mine.

7. This plotline is discussed in greater detail in chapter 3 of *New Monasticism,* "God's Plan to Save the World Through a People," 57–74.

is about participating in the reconciling life of the God who loved his enemies in Jesus Christ. Or, she could tell you that *resurrection* is not just about what happened to Jesus' body after he died and what will happen to ours. More than that, resurrection is *the* sign that new creation has happened.

In the same way that a language is best learned by immersion, it is helpful to consider our role as *language learners* and to think of the Christian life as *learning the gospel by immersion*. Remember: to be "baptized" in the first century meant "to be immersed." Most importantly, it meant for the early Christians being immersed into a person—the person of Jesus Christ.

Consider Romans 6:3–4: "Do you no know that all of us who have been *immersed* into Christ Jesus have been *immersed* into his death? Therefore we have been buried with him by *immersion* into death, so that, just as Christ was raised from the dead by the glory of the Father, so we too might walk in newness of life."

Learning a language by immersion happens through direct contact with another linguistic world and way of life. It is slow (it often takes at least 6–8 months to become conversational); dynamic (there are ups and downs—days when you feel like you could write poetry and others when you can't manage a simple phone call); and challenging (there is the ever-present temptation to "fall back" and express yourself effortlessly in your native language).

Learning the gospel by immersion happens through direct contact with another person/reality—what E. Stanley Jones referred to as the "unchanging person" (Heb. 13:8) and the "unshakable kingdom" (Heb. 12:28). Like learning a language, learning the gospel by immersion is also slow, dynamic, and challenging. In fact, it takes a lifetime. Even after being "transferred [and immersed] into the kingdom" (Col. 1:13), we will be tempted to "fall back" on a way of speaking and living that does not depend on the power of God.

However difficult, we know that learning such a language is possible because Jesus comes to us as the kingdom's "native speaker"—the One who speaks the words of God fluently and whose lifestyle is that of complete dependence upon the power of God. The gospel tells us that it is possible to "express ourselves" in terms of a new language and way of life: that the power of God comes to us in Jesus, and trusting in him and learning from him (Matt. 11:28–29) we can learn the language of the gospel by immersion.

In his book, *Renovation of the Heart: Putting on the Character of Christ*, Dallas Willard describes this pattern of growth—and its relevance both to language learning and "learning Christ" (Eph. 4:20)—as the "VIM pattern," whose three basic elements include vision, intention, and means.[8]

You could think of the layout of *New Monasticism* in this way: chapters 1–3 of the book cast the *vision* through signs, stories, and roots; chapter 4 orients our

8. Willard, *Renovation of the Heart*, 85–93.

intention by outlining how to "play the Bible's game"; and the practices described in chapters 5–9 serve as the *means* for cultivating a life together through further experimentation.

If personal growth "in the knowledge and grace of our Lord Jesus Christ" (2 Pet. 3:18) and "building up the church" are two sides of the same coin (the coin being Christ himself), then we need to find ways to join our "personal spiritual disciplines" with "collective spiritual disciplines." Only in this way will we be able to focus our *vision* on a new way of life in which we *intend together* to become apprentices of Jesus by engaging in certain *means*, learning to live with him and/as his friends in the kingdom of God. The practices are the means that put us into direct contact with other members of the body of Christ and immerse us into the reality of the gospel of the Kingdom of God.

3) Pilgrims

To become language learners for the sake of telling God's story is, finally, to discover that we are a pilgrim people. As *pilgrims*, we have to learn what it means that we belong to a community that is "on the way" and "in the way"—that is, on a journey with the risen Christ. In John's gospel, Jesus makes two statements that place his followers on a journey with him. "I have called you friends. . . . You did not choose me but I chose you" (John 15:15–16). "As the Father has sent me, so I send you" (John 20:21).

Of course, we are all deeply formed according to "where we are from"—our homeland. But in the Bible, a genuine homeland is something *promised* to God's people. What marks Israel's identity more than "where they are from" is that they have been "called out" and "sent" by God. Moreover, Christians live on this side of the paradigm shift that is *resurrection*. So, we have a new *we* (a new social identity) and a new *way* (of speaking and living together) as we move toward the fullness of a new *world* (the new creation in Christ). Living into the new *we*, the new *way*, and the new *world* is what it means to say that we are *pilgrims*.

This means that we need not fear entering into the same process that Abraham, Ruth, and Paul (among others) had to undergo—moving to a new land and learning their ways and their language in order to be God's witnesses there. But it also means that we learn what it means to be "sent" even as we "stay." The Great Commission in Matthew 28 is best translated: "*going*, make disciples." Which is to say, wherever you find yourself, make disciples. Remember: when the risen Christ encounters the two disciples on the road to Emmaus, *he sends them back to where they came from* in order to be his witnesses there (Luke 24:49).

G. K. Chesterton captures this notion of *pilgrimage* in a lovely way as he tells the story of an English yachtsman who set out to sail the seas, miscalculated, and ended up "discovering England." Yet upon returning to where he had begun his journey, he finds his starting point to be familiar, yet strange. According to Chesterton, the point is this: "How can we contrive to be at once astonished at the world and yet at home in it?... how can this world give us at once the fascination of a strange town and the comfort and honour of being our own town?"[9]

Yet, perhaps "pilgrim" does not capture everything that is at stake with this paradigm shift. Given the current challenge that the immigration question brings to the U.S. church, we might ask what it could mean to see ourselves as *immigrants*—those who are "strangers and foreigners on the earth" (Heb. 11:13) and those who have been granted citizenship in a land to which we don't belong by birth (Phil. 2:20), but where we have the "legal" right to stay because God "has rescued us from the power of darkness and *immigrated* us into the kingdom of his beloved Son" (Col. 1:13).

FINDING OUR PLACE IN THE CIRCLE

To begin thinking about ourselves as a community of apprentices, let's consider an image that comes from a fourth-century monk, Dorotheos of Gaza. It is the image of a *circle* that portrays the inseparability of the Great Commandment to love God and neighbor (Matt. 23:37–39). In her book *To Pray and To Love*, Roberta Bondi describes Dorotheos's circle in the following way:

> Imagine . . . that we have drawn a circle with a compass. God is at the center, where the point of the compass went. Now imagine that the outside of the circle is the world, and the lives of human beings are represented by many straight lines drawn from the outside to the center. Notice how you follow a single line from the outside toward God, all the lines come closer together. This is the way human beings relate to God and to each other. . . . The diagram works in reverse as well. If you follow a single line from the center out to the edge again, you notice that all the lines become farther apart as they go away from the center. . . . We cannot love God and hate or even be indifferent to our neighbor. Growth in the love of God also has to include love of those images of God with whom we share the world.[10]

---

9. Chesterton, *Orthodoxy*, 12.

10. Bondi, *To Pray and to Love*, 31–32.

Use the space below to sketch the circle and the double-movement toward God and neighbor:

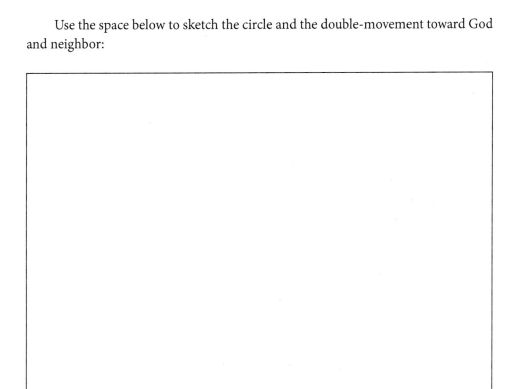

So, how might this circle focus our vision to read the "signs of the times"? If the "signs that's it hard to be Christian" are indicative of forces that threaten to pull us further away from our neighbors and from God, then the "signs of something new" is the resurrection sign—the sign that in the midst of sin and death the gospel is nevertheless the "power of God unto salvation" (Rom. 1:16).

So, think of the circle as a visual prompt to recall what Wilson-Hartgrove claims at the end of the first chapter: "Once we realize that it's hard to be Christian in America, it's easier to remember that none of us can do it on our own. We need each other, and we need God. We need the same power that raised Jesus from the dead. The good news is that even amidst the fragments of the church we're called to be, we have that power" (21).

The upshot is this: Jesus is risen and present in the circle as "the one *mediator* between God and humankind" (1 Tim. 2:5)—the one who is not only in the circle but the one who is "in-between" all the persons in the circle, mediating and reconciling them to one another. If we drop the above quote inside the circle, it helps us remember the truth of the resurrection: nothing can separate us from the love of God, and therefore, from our neighbors. And if we find our place inside the circle, we will begin to see ourselves as not just "fragments of the church" but as "living stones" (1 Pet. 2:5) that are being "built together spiritually into a dwelling place for God"

(Eph. 2:22). So, to find our place within the circle is to "let [our]selves be built into a spiritual house, to be a holy priesthood, to offer spiritual sacrifices acceptable to God through Jesus Christ" (1 Pet. 2:5).

HOSTING THE SESSIONS

Before moving on to Part 2 and the sessions themselves, I would like to borrow an expression from jazz music and suggest that we think of each group session as a "jam session." In this analogy, the participants are the *musicians*—those who have to come to play their instruments with others in order to "jam"—that is, to make music together. The teacher/leader takes on the dual role of *arranger* and *bandleader*.

Before a musical event or "gig," the arranger thinks through and organizes the musical elements: Which songs shall we play? Which instruments would go well with these songs? Which keys should they be played in? Where is this session going to take place? In the same way, the group session arranger will be in charge of selecting the themes to be discussed, the resources to be employed, and the sequence in which the session will proceed.

During the "jam session" the bandleader may also be a musician who leads and plays his instrument at the same time. Or the bandleader may contribute to the music by her silence and the gestures she makes to lead others to stay "in time," to focus, and to work together to create something that is more than the sum of its parts. At any rate, the bandleader knows that less is more, and that her primary role is not to play a lot of notes, but rather to build others up so they can play them together.

To carry the analogy just a bit further (stay with me!): during a "jam session" jazz musicians tend to play from "lead sheets" that include just the key signature, tempo, chord changes, and the melody line of the song. These "lead sheets" are often taken from "fake books," because it *looks like* the musicians are all playing what is written out in the score. Of course, anyone who has tried to join in a jam session knows that "faking it" is hardly what's going on. The musicians are actually dipping into their musical "bag"—the sum total of their *prior* development of a collection of musical phrases that may be drawn on at any time. What really happens in the session is something like this: the bandleader calls a tune, the musicians grab their lead sheets, and from these common musical elements and from their "bag," they begin to "jam" or improvise, as they freely play with *and* off one another within the given constraints of the arrangement. That's the jam session! And that is what's ahead in Part 2.

PART TWO

GETTING STARTED: KNOWING WHERE WE ARE

One of the most important things we can do as we get started with the sessions is to make our expectations clear to ourselves and to the group. Begin by responding to these two questions.

Why have you committed yourself to this course?

_____

_____

_____

_____

_____

_____

_____

_____

_____

_____

_____

_____

_____

_____

What do you hope to get out of our time together?

_____

_____

_____

_____

_____

_____

_____

_____

_____

_____

_____

_____

_____

_____

VOCABULARY EXERCISE

Recalling the point made earlier about conversion and the acquisition of new language skills, the following exercise is designed for participants to pay more attention to how they use the language of faith, as well as to clear some space for the session work. It is likely that during participation in the group sessions, you will end up struggling to articulate what you mean to say, and that's all right. But the exercise is placed here as *preparation* for the sessions, so that key terms have already been examined, opening up the possibility for greater fluency.

Don't worry about giving the "right" answer. Your comments should aim less at giving a *definition* for the words, but rather at *describing* how you use these words and try to relate them to the context of your community of faith. How do you understand the *function* of these words in the Christian life?

Tip: Date your comments in the margin, and begin to include other scripture references that are related to the term. Pay attention to how your language use changes over time. As this takes place, continue to add future comments below, dating them as well.

Example: Conversion

From that time Jesus began to proclaim, "*Repent*, for the kingdom of heaven has come near" (Matt. 4:17).

> "Now there was a man from the Pharisees named Nicodemus, a member of the Jewish ruling council. He came to Jesus at night and said, 'Rabbi, we know you are a teacher who has come from God. For no one could perform the miraculous signs you are doing if God were not with him.' In reply Jesus declared, "I tell you the truth, no one can see the kingdom of God unless he is *born again*"' (John 3:1–3).

Conversion has to do with the ongoing changes that take place in the life of a disciple as a result of pledging allegiance to Jesus and his kingdom. In conversion, God's grace enables us (1) to renarrate our life stories around a new social identity (i.e., "I'm no longer just a white guy, but a gentile Christian."); (2) to learn a new language—a new way to talk about self, world, and God; and (3) to undergo a paradigm shift that sees the world in light of Christ's resurrection and the gift of a new creation. It opens up a new way of living and requires a break with the old ways of sin and death. (12/27/07) Conversion is a terrorist like Paul becoming an evangelist, or a crook like Zaccheus becoming generous. (12/29/07)

Gospel

"For I am not ashamed of the *gospel*; it is the power of God for salvation to everyone who has faith, to the Jew first and also to the Greek" (Rom. 1:16).

"And this *gospel* of the kingdom will be preached in the whole world as a testimony to all nations, and then the end will come" (Matt. 24:14).

Comments: _____
_____
_____
_____
_____
_____
_____
_____
_____
_____
_____
_____

Kingdom of God

"The time has come," he said. "The *kingdom of God* is near. Repent and believe the good news!" (Mark 1:15).

"For the *kingdom of God* is not food and drink but righteousness and peace and joy in the Holy Spirit" (Romans 14:17).

"Your kingdom is *an everlasting kingdom*; your dominion endures throughout all ages" (Psalm 145:13).

Comments: _____
_____
_____
_____
_____
_____
_____
_____
_____
_____
_____

Disciple

"Then Jesus said to the Jews who had believed in him, 'If you continue in my word, you are truly my *disciples*; and you will know the truth, and the truth will make you free'" (John 8:31–32).

"I give you a new commandment, that you love one another. Just as I have loved you, you also should love one another. By this everyone will know that you are my *disciples*, if you have love for one another" (John 13:34–35).

"Come to me, all you that are weary and carrying heavy burdens, and I will give you rest. Take my yoke upon you, and *learn from me*; for I am gentle and humble of heart, and you will find rest for your souls. For my yoke is easy and my burden is light" (Matt. 11:28–29).

"He called the crowd with his *disciples*, and said to them, 'If any want to become my *followers*, let them deny themselves and take up their cross and follow me. For those who want to save their life will lose it, and those who lose their life for my sake, and for the sake of the gospel, will save it'" (Mark 8:34–35).

Comments: _____

_____

_____

_____

_____

_____

_____

_____

_____

_____

_____

Grace

"For by grace you have been saved through faith, and this is not your own doing; it is the gift of God—not the result of works, so that no one may boast. For we are what he has made us in Christ Jesus for good works, which God prepared beforehand to be our way of life" (Eph. 2:8–10).

"For you know the grace of our Lord Jesus Christ, that though he was rich, yet for your sakes he became poor, so that by his poverty you might become rich" (2 Cor. 8:9).

"But grow in the grace and knowledge of our Lord and Savior Jesus Christ" (2 Pet. 3:18).

Comments: _____

_____

_____

_____

_____

_____

_____

_____

_____

_____

_____

_____

Holiness

"[A]s [God] who has called you is holy, be holy yourselves in all your conduct; for it is written, 'You shall *be holy, as I am holy*'" (1 Pet 1:15–16, quoting Lev. 11:44).

"But now that you have been set free from sin and have become slaves to God, the benefit you reap leads to *holiness*, and the result is eternal life" (Rom. 6:22).

Comments: _____

_____

_____

_____

_____

_____

_____

_____

_____

_____

Church

"And I tell you that you are Peter, and on this rock I will build *my church*, and the gates of Hades will not overcome it" (Matt. 16:18).

"His intent was that now, through *the church*, the manifold wisdom of God should be made known to the rulers and authorities in heavenly realms, according to his eternal purpose which he accomplished in Christ Jesus our Lord" (Eph. 3:10–11).

Comments: _____

_____

_____

_____

_____

_____

_____

_____

_____

Koinonia

"They devoted themselves to the apostles' teaching and to the *koinonia*, to the breaking of bread and the prayers" (Acts 2:42).

"The cup of blessing that we bless, is it not a *koinonia* in the blood of Christ? The bread that we break, is it not a *koinonia* in the body of Christ?" (1 Cor. 10:16).

"We declare to you what we have seen and heard so that you also may have *koinonia* with us; and truly our *koinonia* is with the Father and with his Son Jesus Christ" (1 John 1:13).

Comments: _____

_____

_____

_____

_____

_____

_____

_____

_____

WHAT? SO WHAT? NOW WHAT?

The rest of Part 2 provides the resources for the session work. While there is freedom to arrange, cut out, repeat, add others resources, etc., it will be helpful to keep in mind that the sessions should ideally have a certain movement to them. Remember that the movement is toward "learning to live together the way God made us to live." Here are three general questions to be considered for the arrangement of the sessions to enhance our involvement in this "experiential learning" process: What? So What? Now What?[1]

(1) "What?" sets up the central claim of the session through *learning hooks* such as Scripture, students' prior knowledge/experience/practices, stories, reflections and guiding questions on the reading, etc., that aim to stimulate and open up new learning and insights. It invites the participants to ask:

> *Which practices and/or ways of living are being described, advocated, or challenged here?*

(2) "So What?" relates the reflection to "where we are," in order for us to receive the gospel—as Walker Percy put it—not as "information" but as "news." (If you are not sure about that distinction, say to yourself, "My house is on fire." Or: "My wife is pregnant." And now ask yourself, Is that just information, or is it news?) So, the second component invites the participants to ask:

> *How does "X" connect with my/our life? What kind of life together is possible given that "X" (e.g., the resurrection) is the case?*

(3) "Now What?" completes the session through activities and suggestions that lead the participants to ask and respond to the question:

> *How do we begin to organize ourselves and plan strategically in order to "go and do likewise"? Or: How do we now "learn to live together the way God made us to live"?*

---

1. The use of these three questions is an adaption of the approach found in Barbara Bruce's *Start Here: Teaching and Learning With Adults*.

Notice how Paul's argument that culminates in Philippians 4 integrates these three questions:

(1) **What?** Jesus is Lord and there is no other: "Jesus Christ is Lord, to the glory of God the Father" (Phil. 2:11).

(2) **So what?** Our life-context is transformed as we interact with his presence and power: "The Lord is near. Do not worry about in anything, but in everything, by prayer and supplication with thanksgiving let your requests by made known to God. And the peace of God, which surpasses all understanding, will guard your hearts and your minds in Christ Jesus" (Phil. 4:4–7).

(3) **Now what?** We learn from one another how to know Christ Jesus and share his life: "Keep on doing the things that you have learned and received and heard and seen in me, and the God of peace will be with you." (Phil. 4:9)

CHAPTER 1

READING THE SIGNS OF THE TIMES

Reflection Questions

One of the basic claims of the first chapter is that "it's hard to be Christian in America" (6). Give a reason for why you agree or disagree with that claim.

_____
_____
_____
_____
_____
_____
_____
_____
_____

Describe specifically how the five "signs that it's hard to be Christian" *signify* a way of life that resists the power of the resurrection and/or is in open rebellion against God's reign "on earth as it is in heaven." It may be helpful to return to Dorotheos of Gaza's "circle" which portrays the inseparability of love of God and love of neighbor.[1]

_____
_____
_____
_____
_____
_____
_____
_____
_____

In medical lingo, a sign is an indication of state/quality of health. Often medical signs are not readily perceived or have no apparent meaning for the patient, yet their significance is grasped by the physician's powers of observation. In light of this chapter's

1. See above, Part 1, 10–11.

diagnosis—namely, that it's hard to be Christian in America—are there any other "signs of the time" that you would add that confirm this diagnosis?

_____

_____

_____

_____

_____

_____

_____

_____

_____

Wilson-Hartgrove writes: "we can see more clearly than ever before, perhaps, just how hard it is for any of us to pledge our ultimate allegiance to Jesus. *Christian* has become an adjective that we tack on to some more fundamental identity. We don't use the word like they did at Antioch, to describe a peculiar people. We don't use it that way because we can feel how hard it really is to be a Christian in America." (12). How would you describe that "more fundamental identity" on to which "Christian" tends to get tacked (e.g., American, consumer, individual, free citizen, liberal, conservative)?

_____

_____

_____

_____

_____

_____

_____

_____

_____

The author writes: "Once we realize that it's hard to be Christian in America, it's easier to remember that none of us can do it on our own. We need each other, and we need God. We need the same power that raised Jesus from the dead. The good news is that even amidst the fragments of the church we're called to be, we have that power" (21). In light of this quote, consider how we might begin to learn dependence on (1) one another, and (2) the power of God.

_____

_____

_____

_____

_____

_____

_____

_____

_____

"Theology is done with the Bible in one hand and the newspaper in the other." (Karl Barth). What do you make of this statement? How do we hold them together? Do you find that the time spent with the newspaper (or other news media like CNN) exposes you to what this chapter calls the "signs of the times"? Do you find that your Bible reading helps you "read" the same world described in the newspaper? Or do you often sense the Bible describes a world in which you don't live?

_____

_____

_____

_____

_____

_____

_____

_____

_____

Evaluate the time you spend with the newspaper/Internet/other news media and the Bible. Begin by estimating how much time you spend per day with each. Do you think that being intentional about "reading the signs of the times" means that we should spend as much time with the Word as we do with the words that we see and hear in the news media?

_____

_____

_____

_____

_____

_____

_____

_____

Suggested Exercises

Chapter 1 points to five "signs of the times"—five signs that it's hard to be Christian in America:

(1) war-making (15)
(2) the color line (15–16)
(3) immigration (16–17)
(4) abortion (17)
(5) billboards (17–18)

On a scale from 1 to 10 (10 being the greatest impact) rank each of the signs according to its direct impact upon you? your congregation? your city/town?

The story goes that when asked about why she only carried a Bible around with her when there are so many other good books to read, a woman replied, "Why just the Bible? Because it's the only book that reads *me*." Can you relate to that?

The book of Jonah can easily be read in one sitting. Take ten minutes to read it straight through, reading it from the "outsider" perspective of a Ninevite. Reflect on how you hear and receive the prophet's message of judgment and hope with these quotes in mind:

(1) "'Forty days more, and Nineveh will be *over*turned'—or turned *around* (Jonah 3:4 NIV) Nineveh was about to be either destroyed or converted. It could mean either one. The paradoxical prophet proclaimed a message of judgment and hope at the same time. The end of the world as they know it in Nineveh was also the beginning of something new. In the ruins of an old life lay the promise of new life with God" (19–20).

(2) "This is a book about what it means to be Christian as citizens of the world's last remaining superpower at the beginning of the third millenium" (21).

(3) "Repent—not because you must, but because you may" (Karl Barth).

Use this space to record your own questions and reflections.

_____
_____
_____
_____
_____
_____

CHAPTER 2

SEEING SIGNS OF SOMETHING NEW

Reflection Questions

Consider the following quote: "The point of any revolution is to turn things around—to change the world that is into the world that ought to be" (32). Do you tend to the think of the kingdom of God as a revolution, or as a reformation movement? Do you think of Jesus more as a "revolutionary" or a "reformer"?

_____

_____

_____

_____

_____

_____

_____

_____

The author compares the kingdom of God to rhizomes, whose root structure allows for extended growth beneath the ground, even though it does not impose itself as a formidable presence. God's revolution is "the 'quiet revolution' . . . [that] doesn't spring up big and tall, parading its supremacy over all the other kingdoms of the earth. Instead, it spreads underground. It thrives beneath the surface. When you whack some little piece off, it just spreads somewhere else. And in the end, God's kingdom wins" (33). If this is the case, then the question is not whether the kingdom is growing but where? Comment on where you have seen new signs of the kingdom? Where have you seen the kingdom's vines spreading out? Has it tended to be "below the radar"?

_____

_____

_____

_____

_____

_____

_____

_____

Which stories or signs seemed to stir your imagination? How so?

_____

_____

_____

_____

_____

_____

_____

In the section "Searching for St. Benedict" (36–39), the author relates the Benedictine "quiet revolution" in the midst of the fragmentation of the Roman Empire to new monasticism's emergence in the midst of the widespread fragmentation of the contemporary church in the American context. Do you find that connection helpful?

_____

_____

_____

_____

_____

_____

_____

Suggested Exercises

- Wilson-Hartgrove describes new monasticism as "a river of faithfulness" (see 26–34) that has been flowing for some 80 years. This river joins together older communities—Bruderhof, Catholic Worker, Koinonia Farms, CCDA—as well as newer ones that are emerging and joining themselves to the river's wider and older flow: "By God's grace they could see that they weren't starting something new, but that they had fallen into a river of faithfulness which flows on to join other tributaries as it finds its way to the future God has given us" (33–34)

  Use a map or a globe and try "mapping" the "river of faithfulness" described above. Begin with Germany, then New York City, Georgia, and Mississippi. Then add to that other communities that form other tributaries. Where do you see yourself in relation to the river: caught up in its stream? Or: standing by its edge wanting to fall in?

- Designate someone to be a scribe to write on a board or flipchart. Then do a "free association" exercise first with "revolution" and then with "reformation." Say anything that comes to mind! (Example: "Revolution" . . . you know, the Beatles' song.)

- Read John 9. Consider how signs Jesus performed were met with both sight and blindness. Would you say that this passage confirms the saying, "believing is seeing"?

- The author writes, "We need to be reminded that God is always doing a new thing, always breathing new life into the church. If we have eyes to see, there are signs of something new right alongside the signs of the time" (37). Take a look at the "12 Marks of a New Monasticism" (39). Pick one and reflect on it as a practice in sowing the seeds of a "gospel realism."

Use this space to record your own questions and reflections.

_____

_____

_____

_____

_____

_____

_____

CHAPTER 3

A VISION SO OLD IT LOOKS NEW

Reflection Questions

What comes to mind when you think of the term *monasticism*? Are your associations primarily positive or negative? What about *new monasticism*? How has reading this book changed the way you think about both terms?

_____

_____

_____

_____

_____

_____

_____

_____

If we define a monastic as "one who gives him/herself fully to God," do you think that's a helpful description for all baptized Christians?

_____

_____

_____

_____

_____

_____

_____

_____

Movements and revolutions use mottos to distill their vision. Do you find "to pray and to work" to be a compelling motto for a revolution or an "alternative society"?

_____

_____

_____

_____

_____

_____

_____

_____

Benedict envisioned the monastery as a "school for the Lord's service," and his *Rule* "offered a model for communities where people could live a life of prayer together, serving one another and the community around them [by] 'be[ing] the change they seek'" (47). What do you find attractive or captivating about such a vision for the Christian life? Does it sound novel? Out-dated? Or "so old that it's new"?

_____

_____

_____

_____

_____

_____

_____

_____

_____

Suggested Exercises

- In Philippians 4:9, Paul writes, "Keep on doing the things that you have learned and received and heard and seen in me, and the God of peace with be with you." (Translation: "Do what I do, not just what I say—and it will go well with you!") Think of your "favorite" saint—biblical, canonical, or local—who helps you "run the race with perseverance" and "look to Jesus." What truth have you learned, received, heard, and/or seen incarnated in their life that you would like to keep on doing?

- Get a copy of the book, *Cloud of Witnesses*, edited by Jim Wallis and Joyce Hollyday. Each chapter profiles a different saint among the great "cloud of witnesses"—several of whom are highlighted here in chapter 3 as new monastics. The editors describe the significance of these witnesses by placing them in line with biblical saints that came before them:

  > Hebrews 11:4 begins the 'roll call of faith,' mentioning by name Noah, Abraham, Sarah, Isaac, Moses, Rahab, and other. This is not a gallery of success and accomplishment; these are not winners and world shakers. Most of them wouldn't be called successful by any standard. But they kept the faith. And so they are remembered. . . . This passage is our family tree. Here are listed men and women who have gone before and blazed the trail for us. Here are our foremothers and forefathers, the ones on whose shoulders we now stand.[1]

  Now begin to design your local's church "family tree"—or "family river with tributaries." Reflect on how "falling into the river of faithfulness" is primarily a matter of catching a vision for a new way of life *through other witnesses* and giving oneself over to that new way.

- Share how you have observed signs of "Christ's technique" at work—that is, the "trickle-up" effect of the gospel of the kingdom of God.

Use this space to record your own questions and reflections.

_____

_____

_____

_____

_____

_____

1. Wallis and Hollyday, *Cloud of Witnesses*, xv.

CHAPTER 4

GOD'S PLAN TO SAVE THE WORLD THROUGH A PEOPLE

Reflection Questions

Which "game"—"Make Myself," "Make Yourself," or "God Makes a People"—best describes how you have learned to read the Bible? Have you ever had a nagging sense that you were playing the wrong "game" with the Bible?

_____

_____

_____

_____

_____

_____

_____

_____

_____

Wilson-Hartgrove writes, "God gave the Law to Israel not only to show them a way to live, but also to remind them that they were a people set apart" (65). Do you think your church is more identifiable/recognizable by what it does not do or by what it does? By the "shall nots" or the "shalls"?

_____

_____

_____

_____

_____

_____

_____

_____

Some friends who live in a new monastic community tell the story of how their charism for hospitality and their desire to live simply began to conflict with one another. That is, they would regularly have neighborhood friends over for dinner, but soon recognized that serving vegetarian and even "dumpstered" food items did not come across as "hospitality" to their neighbors who were used to fried chicken or at least a portion or meat that had not seen a trash can. So the community decided to do a Bible study about food. One of the outcomes of the study was the decision to eat vegetarian and "dumpstered" food on their "house nights" and serve meat or a meat substitute when guests were invited. This kind of collective discernment is one example of what it looks like to read the Bible in community. Share your experiences on reading and "practicing" the Bible in community. What's the difference between reading the Bible in community and simply having a "group Bible study"?

_____
_____
_____
_____
_____
_____
_____
_____
_____
_____

The following quote points to what's at stake in reading the Bible in community: "every church needs to figure out how to help its people play the Bible's game. If Scripture isn't meant to help us play Make Myself or Make Yourself but instead is about the game called God Makes a People, *how can our churches help everyone learn to play the game we were made for?*" (71, emphasis mine). The author makes a few suggestions about how this can be done in our local congregation through (1) paying attention to how/what we teach our children, (2) the small group movement, and (3) higher commitment membership. What practices are already in place in your church that facilitate playing the Bible's game?

_____
_____
_____
_____
_____
_____
_____
_____
_____

Suggested Exercises

- One way to enter more deeply into the "thought experiment" described on page 58 is by organizing a "role play" debate. In this debate, however, one does not argue one's own position, but rather the one assigned to them (important detail!). Select a moderator, and then divide the groups into the three teams. Each team will argue its case as a response to the question: "What game does the Bible give us instructions for?" Team 1 argues for "Make Myself"; Team 2 for "Make Yourself"; Team 3 for "God Makes a People." Each team will argue that its position most adequately and coherently describes how to play the Bible's game. To make things interesting, let's assume that each team will have to interact with at least the three following books of the Bible: Genesis, Matthew, and Ephesians.

- "God's Plan A looks like saving the world through a people. . . . Maybe God's plan B is to save the world through personal relationships with individuals. . . . When we look closely, the authors of the New Testament seem to go to great lengths to say that God doesn't have a Plan B" (67–68). Go back to the "circle" described in the introduction. Does the circle help you grasp what Plan A looks like? Just out of curiosity: How would you draw Plan B?

- "I used to believe the Bible was mostly an instruction manual for how to get right with God and be a good person. . . . But if the Bible is a story about God's plan to save the world *through a people*, then my salvation and sanctification depend on finding my true home with God's people. Apart from the story of this people, I can't have a relationship with God" (58). Does "God's plan to save the world through a people" strike you as a helpful "one-liner" about the Bible's plot line? Imagine that you have ten minutes to tell someone what the Bible is about. How would you describe the "big picture"? Which passages would be key for you? Begin practicing your way of telling the "Bible's game" in an abridged way that is still coherent.

Use this space to record your own questions and reflections.

_____

_____

_____

_____

_____

_____

_____

CHAPTER 5

RELOCATION AND RENEWAL

Reflection Questions

Here are two questions straight out of the book: "What could it mean to re-imagine church from the margins of our cities and towns? How might God's desert vision inform our mission and life together in congregations?" (84–85)

_____

_____

_____

_____

_____

_____

_____

The author describes the monastics as those who "needed to see the world from a different place if they were going to see it anew. So they moved. And when they did, they started movements. The renewal of the church depended on relocation" (77). In light of this quote, consider the following as a vision for revival in the local church: the revival of our local churches depends less on styles of worship (or even more worship services) and more on our willingness to relocate in order to be with, and learn from, those on the margins.

_____

_____

_____

_____

_____

_____

_____

Read Matthew 25:31–46. Reread verses 35–36: "for I was hungry and you gave me food, I was thirsty and you gave me something to drink, I was a stranger and you welcomed me, I was naked and you gave me clothing, I was sick and you took care of me, _I was in prison and you visited me._" Now reread verse 40: "And the king will answer, 'Truly I tell you, just as you did it to one of the least of these who are members of my family, *you did it to me.*" How have you encountered Jesus in the faces of those who suffer? Would you say that we encounter Christ in our neighbor, and *especially* in our neighbors who are suffering?

A man recalls an occasion in which he received a phone call the night before going to preach at a men's prison. The friend who called said, "I just remembered that you're preaching at the prison tomorrow. Tell Jesus I said hello when you see him tomorrow." Where have you been to serve your neighbor and ended up meeting Jesus too?

Latin America theologian Orlando Costas often referred to Jesus' own tactics of "relocation and renewal" in terms of the "Galilean option" and "going outside the gate" (Heb. 13). For Costas, these are shorthand descriptions of how Jesus organized his ministry as a movement from the periphery to the center. How do these descriptions combine with Israel's "desert vision" to illumine our understanding of relocating? How do they help with reimagining the church's role to make known God's mystery (Eph. 3:9–11) "from the margins"?

_____

_____

How does the new monastic vision for relocation and renewal offer an alternative to "spiritual Reagonomics" on the one hand and a social gospel of uplift and empowerment on the other? What exactly does relocation make possible?

_____

_____

_____

_____

_____

_____

_____

_____

How can your church begin to experiment with "Getting the Word Out"? Where? Who are the Ann Atwaters in your congregation or in your community?

_____

_____

_____

_____

_____

_____

_____

_____

Suggested Exercises

- Make a list of some "deserts"—abandoned spaces where God still dwells and which God still uses as a teaching ground—that you have visited. What did you learn there? What did you begin to reimagine?

- Read Exodus 3:1—4:17 and pay attention to the Moses' five reasons for why he is not the guy to lead Israel out of Egypt. How you ever found yourself using these excuses as your own?

- Revisit the five "signs that it's hard to be a Christian" described in chapter 1 (14–18) and ponder how relocation helps you to see them and the world and to "reimagine your role within it" (77).

Use this space to record your own questions and reflections.

_____

_____

_____

_____

_____

_____

_____

_____

_____

_____

_____

_____

_____

_____

_____

_____

_____

_____

_____

_____

_____

_____

_____

_____

CHAPTER 6

DAILY BREAD AND FORGIVEN DEBTS

Reflection Questions

Has there been a time when you have experienced God's "economics of providence"—a time in which God's abundance trumped the logic of scarcity?

_____

_____

_____

_____

_____

_____

_____

_____

_____

Read 2 Corinthians 8–9. Notice the repetition of the words "grace" (Greek: charis) and "gift" (Greek: charism). How would you describe the relationship between "grace" and "gift" here in Paul's argument.

_____

_____

_____

_____

_____

_____

_____

_____

A pastor in the Dominican Republic refers to the "feeding miracle" in Matthew 14 as "The 5 and 2 principle." He suggests that the heart of the miracle was getting the disciples to let go of what they had in order to meet the needs of those around them. The miracle, he says, is not that they gave out of their abundance to meet others' need, but that their obedience to the command "You give them something to eat," allowed God's abundance to multiply what they lacked. Reread Matthew 14:13–

21. What do you find miraculous about this scene? (Check out the video clip at: www.theworkofthepeople.com/index.php?ct=store.details&pid=V00292)

_____

_____

_____

_____

_____

_____

_____

_____

_____

What do think you is more important for our participation in "God's economy": our willingness to interrupt the "filthy rotten system" (Dorothy Day) by becoming generous, or our creating an alternative system to capitalism?

_____

_____

_____

_____

_____

_____

_____

_____

_____

Suggested Exercises

- Read aloud "At a Sacrifice," one of Peter Maurin's "easy essays."[1] How does his description of the early Christians relate to how you would describe your church's practice(s) of sharing?

- Wilson-Hartgrove writes, "the Empire's economy isn't the only possibility. God's economy insists on interrupting the filthy rotten system. And it does it with a celebration. It's what the Old Testament calls a feast. . . . Each celebration was an act of resistance against the power of Mammon" (100). Think about plans for a future feast. Who would you invite to your next redistribution party? Where would it be held?

- Here's another "thought experiment": Let's imagine that someone in your group floats this suggestion: "Why doesn't our local church earmark 10% of its annual budget to provide no-interest loans to its members as a concrete step toward making economic considerations more relational within the church and toward experimenting with the Jubilee announcement of debt-release for the people of God. How does that sound? Any takers?"

- Learn more about Relational Tithe as "a network that makes real economic sharing among God's people possible" (102): www.relationaltithe.org. Share stories and begin to think about how your church can become involved.

- Order copies of Daniel Erlander's *Manna and Mercy: A Brief History of God's Unfolding Promise to Mend the Entire Universe*. Use it as a resource for thinking deeply about God's economy while learning to "play the Bible's game."

Use this space to record your own questions and reflections.

_____
_____
_____
_____
_____
_____
_____
_____
_____
_____
_____

1. Maurin, *Easy Essays*, 110–11.

CHAPTER 7

A NEW PEACE CORPS

Reflection Questions

"If Jesus Christ is indeed the peace of the world, then every church is called to be a peace church as his body. Differences about politics in America ought not to distract us from that primary vocation" (122). Do you agree with this statement?

_____
_____
_____
_____
_____
_____
_____
_____

A wise theology professor once made the comment: "Whenever you come to a problem, give it a story." The author describes the problem of the white-black color line by telling a story: "In Atlanta today it is not just social convention or cultural preference that separates white from black, rich from poor. White and black are separated by a dividing wall of hostility because of a history of violence" (116). What difference does it make to our understanding of the link between sin, violence, and racism, if we give the link a story? Can we understand them without storytelling?

_____
_____
_____
_____
_____
_____
_____
_____

Read Ephesians 2:11–22. Go back to the image of the circle described in the introduction. Does the circle—and the double-movement toward God and neighbor—confirm or illumine the following quote: "Ephesians doesn't just say that peace with our enemies is possible. It says that peace with our enemies is the only way we can have peace with God. . . . You can't have peace with God outside the church that is God's peace. There is no personal relationship with Jesus without a personal relationship with your enemies" (111)?

_____

_____

_____

_____

_____

_____

_____

_____

_____

In Romans 5:10 Paul writes, "For if while we were enemies, we were reconciled to God through the death of his Son, much more surely, having been reconciled, will we be saved by his life." Does it surprise you to think of yourself as God's enemy? Which is harder for you to swallow: that you are God's enemy or your neighbor's enemy? Or: that Christ reconciles you to God or that Christ reconciles you to your neighbor?

_____

_____

_____

_____

_____

_____

_____

_____

_____

Do you find it more difficult to forgive and confess sin to the people you live with or the people you interact with on a more casual basis? Explain.

_____

_____

_____

_____

_____

_____

_____

_____

Suggested Exercises

- The Open Door is described as an interruption of the world's violence. Just before the verses that describe the advent of Christ's peace (Ephesians 2:11–22), we read this: "For we are what [God] has made us, created in Christ Jesus for good works, which God prepared beforehand to be our way of life." Ponder this verse as a promise that God has already prepared good works of peacemaking for those who are in Christ Jesus—all we have to do in order to interrupt the futile works of the world's violence is "get in the way."

- The next time you participate in the Eucharist/Lord's Supper, think of yourself as a reconciled enemy of God and your neighbor—with nothing in between you except the body of Jesus.

- The U.S. military annually recruits thousands of young people to join the Armed Forces. As a step toward making peacemaking more relational in your church and a viable alternative to military enlistment, consider sponsoring two to four young people in your church to be trained to use the "weapons of the Spirit" and enlist for a term in active nonviolence. Reflect on what the issues would be for your church to recruit for a "new peace corps."

Use this space to record your own questions and reflections.

_____

_____

_____

_____

_____

_____

_____

_____

_____

_____

_____

_____

_____

_____

_____

_____

_____

_____

_____

CHAPTER 8

A CULTURE OF GRACE AND TRUTH

Reflection Questions

"The great temptation in community is to imagine that our life together is not like a garden, but instead like a repair shop" (136). Which image best describes you church's vision of ministry: garden or repair shop?

_____
_____
_____
_____
_____
_____
_____

Would you agree that the church's most important work is tending a culture of grace and truth right in the midst of a world fractured by sin and lies?

_____
_____
_____
_____
_____
_____
_____

"I wonder how many people in churches actually know the basic needs of their fellow church members. . . . We rarely talk about how we could meet one another's basic needs. It doesn't often occur to Christians that this is what church is about" (139–140). Along with "one, holy, catholic, and apostolic," does "meeting one another's basic needs" strike you as a basic "mark" of the church?

_____
_____
_____
_____
_____
_____
_____

A friend recalls an occasion in which he arrived for a counseling session with some Christian brothers at a local prison. During the week an argument had taken place over whether the brothers should be watching TV during their "recreation break" at night. At first the counselor thought to himself, "Right, another example of petty legalism." Then he began to hear some brothers open up about how this time was the only opportunity for them to have fellowship with and pray for one another. He recalls that he changed his mind, as he saw that "not watching TV" was a way for the brothers to free themselves up *for* one another. Can you think of other examples in which something maybe "lawful" but not "helpful" for the community (see 1 Cor. 6:12), or when placing restrictions on ourselves in community is the way we cultivate grace? How would you distinguish such *disciplines* from *legalisms*?

_____

_____

_____

_____

_____

_____

_____

_____

_____

_____

Read Ephesians 2:8–10. Dallas Willard has remarked that contemporary Protestants have, for the most part, inherited an understanding of grace that leaves us *passive* in the Christian life—that is, without any clear sense that we can or should do things to cooperate with God. Citing 2 Peter 3:18 ("But *grow* in the grace and knowledge of our Lord and Savior Jesus Christ."), Willard suggests that this verse along with a host of others tells us that we do have something to do, but with this distinction in mind: the opposite of grace is not effort, but merit. So, if we have a clear understanding that we do not do things to *earn* grace, how should we think about responsibility to *grow* in it?

_____

_____

_____

_____

_____

_____

_____

_____

_____

Do you think that the "saints" mentioned throughout the book need(ed) more or less grace to live as they did?

_____

_____

_____

_____

_____

_____

_____

_____

_____

_____

How has your church experimented with "grassroots ecumenism" (132)? What have you learned from other brothers and sisters who do not belong to your own denominational flock?

_____

_____

_____

_____

_____

_____

_____

_____

_____

John 15 describes Jesus as the vine and his Father as the vinegrower or "gardener" who *prunes* those parts of the vine that do not bear fruit, so that the vine will bear even more fruit. If one of the basic ingredients for tending a culture of grace and truth is time and/or availability for one another, think about what things may need to be pruned away in order for your community's garden to bear more fruit.

_____

_____

_____

_____

_____

_____

_____

_____

Suggested Exercises

- The author suggests that footwashing is fundamentally about how we serve one another in obedience to Jesus' example—or: how we take care of "the basic needs of others in a household" (139). List ways that you can begin to serve one another in your church family (i.e., babysitting co-op, lending belongings to those who need them, time-sharing with cars or other appliances). Now get your (or your brother's) feet wet!

- Brainstorm some answers to the following question: "how does a congregation get the love of God deep in its bones and start tending to a culture of grace and truth among its people?" (138)

- As an act of *cultivating* grace, memorize John 13:34–35. Write it in on a note card, or above your door or mirror—do whatever it takes for these two verses to become part of your mental furniture. Use these verses as part of your armor to "stand against the wiles of the devil" (Eph. 6:11). Or to shift to the "garden" metaphor, use these to cultivate/sow seeds of grace and truth. Whenever you find yourself tempted toward being defensive or critical, say these verses first. (It's the same idea as counting to ten, but with Jesus in your face, reorienting you with his "new commandment".) Does calling the verses to mind serve as an antidote to "trying to fix one another"? Share your results with the group.

Use this space to record your own questions and reflections.

_____

_____

_____

_____

_____

_____

_____

_____

_____

_____

_____

_____

_____

_____

_____

CHAPTER 9

WHY NEW MONASTICISM NEEDS THE CHURCH

Reflection Questions

What is the difference between "going to church" and "becoming the church"? Describe what it looks like to "go to church" without "becoming the church"? Describe how you imagine the possibility of "becoming the church" while at the same time having "fewer services"?

_____
_____
_____
_____
_____
_____
_____

Consider what it would mean for the church to become a "new gang . . . [whose] commitments can't be any more abstract than the concrete realities and relationships of a gang" (145). (Example: What would it mean to prepare someone for baptism as initiation into a new gang of Christians?)

_____
_____
_____
_____
_____
_____
_____

John Alexander commonly referred to the contemporary Christian landscape as being marked by "50% churches": those that stress a personal relationship with Jesus and those that see themselves as the bastions of social justice/change. How has new monasticism helped you to imagine what a 100% church would look like?

_____
_____
_____
_____

_____

_____

_____

Do you agree that "outside the church there is no salvation"? (If you disagree, take a shot at describing how salvation is *mediated*?)

_____

_____

_____

_____

_____

_____

_____

In theology, one might distinguish between "personal sin" and "structural sin." Would you apply that distinction to your understanding of grace as well? Do you find the notion of "structural grace" to be a helpful one?

_____

_____

_____

_____

_____

_____

_____

Would you describe yourself as a "para-church" or a "pro-church" Christian? How would you distinguish between the two?

_____

_____

_____

_____

_____

_____

_____

Suggested Exercises

- An excellent resource for "playing the Bible's game" is *Does God Need the Church?* by Gerhard Lohfink. Provocative title, is it not? As a little exercise, how would you answer that question?

- A friend recalls going to Vacation Bible School as a young child and how every morning during the assembly the group would pledge allegiance to the U.S. flag and then to the Christian flag. So right after reciting this:

  "I pledge allegiance to the flag of the United States of America, and to the Republic for which it stands: one nation under God, indivisible, with liberty and justice for all."

  this would be recited:

  "I pledge allegiance to the Christian flag and to the Savior for whose Kingdom it stands: one brotherhood, uniting all Christians in service and in love."

  Ponder what it means for you to pledge allegiance to Jesus Christ and his church? What would you include in a Christian pledge of allegiance? Write yours below:

  _____
  _____
  _____
  _____
  _____
  _____
  _____
  _____
  _____
  _____
  _____
  _____
  _____

- This chapter develops why new monasticism needs the church: "Maybe the most important thing new monasticism has to say to say to the church is that we need her. . . . It may be that this is the truly 'new' thing God is doing through new monasticism" (141). Let's turn that around by interviewing one another with the following questions: Why do *I* need the church? Why does the church need new monasticism? What have you learned about being Christian and being in the church from your engagement with new monasticism?

Use this space to record your own questions and reflections.

_____

_____

_____

_____

_____

_____

_____

_____

_____

_____

_____

_____

EXPERIMENTING WITH FAITH, HOPE, AND LOVE

To say that we are experimenting with faith, hope, and love is another way of saying that we are "testing out" and learning together how to follow Jesus and "continue in his word" (John 8:31). Some of our experiments will directly open up "new forms of faithfulness." Others will show us what we need to learn and what adjustments we need to make for change to occur. But because we are dealing with experiments—and not recipes or formulas—we may not be able to determine how things will turn out before we actually try. As Soren Kierkegaard put it: "Live it forward, and understand it backwards."

Perhaps the most important thing that we can do to "understand it backwards" is to spend time reflecting upon what we have done together. Consider these words from South African pastor Trevor Hudson: "We don't learn from experience, we learn from reflection upon experience."[1] In other words, as we carry out our collective experiments and turn our churches and other local sites into "laboratories for the gospel," we will also need to be intentional about reflecting upon and even writing about what we are learning and still need to learn. Otherwise, we may be busy experimenting, but not building up the church.

Here is a framework for a "lab report"—a way of reflection on the process of what an experiment might look like and where it might lead us:[2]

1. Hudson, *Compassionate Caring*, 59.

2. This "experiential learning" framework is taken from Conde-Frazier, Many Colored Kingdom, 199.

Original perception: Information shaped by our communities.

[EXAMPLE: Some members of a local church begin to comment on the growing incarceration rate in the U.S. and in their city.]

A new experience: New information or a trigger event may lead to discomfort or dissonance. This is the initial connection with the issue.

[EXAMPLE: A group from our local church begins to relocate one of its adult Sunday School classes by visiting a nearby prison/correctional facility every other week, worshipping with their Christian brothers, learning their stories, studying the Bible with them, and praying with them after worship.

Appraisal: Self-examination, identification, or clarification of the concern. What is going on here (with this situation and inside of me)? How were views or beliefs about this issue constructed? This is a place of deeper encounter with the issue.

[EXAMPLE: The local church begins to explore the connections between Jesus' ministry "to the captives" (Luke 4:18) and the prisoners of our time (Matt. 25:36). The church now has a "live question" before it: Given that the body of Christ is both "free in society" and "behind bars," how can we build up this body together?]

Exploration: Exploring new and old assumptions. Where might this lead me? Testing the veracity of the new.

[EXAMPLE: The church begins to organize a program of service and visitation at the prison as well as transportation/hospitality for those brothers who have "day passes" to worship in local churches on Sundays. The church invites their "guests" to give their testimonies and do some teaching around what they are learning about the gospel.]

Support: Dialogue with others to develop a sense of security and confidence within the new. Seeking the encouragement of family and friends. Feedback is sought as one expresses new ideas and asks for comments. As one comes to new understandings, one also needs new symbols.

[EXAMPLE: Through these new relationships and input from local social workers, the church learns that one of the biggest problems for ex-convicts is not Christian community and fellowship "on the inside," but finding a "new gang" on the outside. The church invites a local worker to do a training workshop on re-entry and prison after-care.]

Continuous questions and challenges: At this point, one begins to see with new eyes, to encounter new stories, and to engage in deeper dialogue. One acts according to one's new understandings, views, and beliefs.

[EXAMPLE: By relocating one of its Sunday School classes "to the margins," the church has encountered Christ in the suffering neighbor, has become aware of how this encounter might shape its mission and life together, and has mobilized the church to build up the "fragments of the church" inside and outside prison into one local gang of Christians. Now it is beginning to ask another question: How does our life together nurture a culture of grace and truth that makes it easier to be good and makes it harder for young people to see prison as their future destiny?]

Remember: we know that we can take the risk of experimentation because we have everything we need—each other, God, and the promise of "the same power that raised Jesus from the dead" (18):

"Now to him who by the power at work within us is able to accomplish abundantly far more that we can ask or imagine, to him be glory in the church and in Christ Jesus to all generations, forever and ever. Amen." (Eph. 3:20)

THE LAB REPORT: NOTES FOR FUTURE EXPERIMENTS

Original perception: _____
_____
_____
_____
_____
_____
_____
_____
_____
_____
_____

A new experience: _____
_____
_____
_____
_____
_____
_____
_____
_____
_____
_____

Appraisal: _____
_____
_____
_____
_____
_____
_____
_____
_____
_____

Exploration: _____

_____
_____
_____
_____
_____
_____
_____
_____
_____
_____
_____

Support: _____

_____
_____
_____
_____
_____
_____
_____
_____
_____
_____

Continuous questions and challenges: _____

_____
_____
_____
_____
_____
_____
_____
_____
_____
_____

WORKS CITED

Bondi, Roberta. *To Pray and to Love*. Minneapolis: Fortress, 1991.

Bonhoeffer, Dietrich. *Life Together/Prayerbook of the Bible*. Minneapolis: Fortress, 1996.

Bruce, Barbara. *Start Here: Teaching and Learning With Adults*. Nashville: Discipleship Resources, 2000.

Chesterton, G. K. *Orthodoxy*. Vancouver: Regent College Publishing, 2004.

Conde-Frazier, Elizabeth. *A Many Colored Kingdom: Multicultural Dynamics for Spiritual Formation*. Grand Rapids: Baker, 2004.

Erlander, Daniel. *Manna and Mercy: A Brief History of God's Unfolding Promise to Mend the Entire Universe*. Minneapolis: Fortress, 1992.

Hudson, Trevor. *Compassionate Caring: A Daily Pilgrimage of Pain and Hope*. Guilford, Surrey: Eagle, 1999.

Lohfink, Gerhard. *Does God Need the Church?: Toward a Theology of the People of God*. Translated by Linda M. Maloney. Collegeville, MN: Liturgical, 1999.

Maurin, Peter. *Easy Essays*. Franciscan Herald, 1984.

Wallis, Jim, and Joyce Hollyday, editors. *Cloud of Witnesses*. Maryknoll, NY: Orbis, 2005.

Willard, Dallas. *Renovation of the Heart: Putting on the Character of Christ*. NavPress, 2002.

Wilson-Hartgrove, Jonathan. *New Monasticism: What It Has to Say To Today's Church*. Grand Rapids: Brazos, 2008.

GOING DEEPER: A READING LIST

Barker, Ashley. *Collective Witness: A Theology and Praxis for a Missionary Order*. Urban Neighbours of Hope, 2000.

Bernard, Jack. *How to Become a Saint*. Brazos, 2007.

Claiborne, Shane. *The Irresistible Revolution*. Zondervan, 2006.

Colwell, Matthew. *Sabbath Economics: Household Practices*. The Church of the Saviour, 2007).

Conde-Frazier, Elizabeth, S. Steve Kang, and Gary A. Parrett, *A Many Colored Kingdom: Multicultural Dynamics for Spiritual Formation*. Baker Academic, 2004.

Ekblad, Bob. *Reading the Bible With the Damned*. Westminster John Knox, 2005.

Erlander, Daniel. *Manna and Mercy: A Brief History of God's Unfolding Promise to Mend the Entire Universe*. Augsburg Fortress, 1995.

Gutierrez, Gustavo. *We Drink From Our Own Wells*. Orbis, 1985.

Hudson, Trevor. *A Mile in My Shoes*. Abingdon, 2005.

Kinsler, Ross and Gloria. *The Biblical Jubilee and the Struggle for Life*. Orbis, 1999.

Myers, Ched. *The Biblical Vision of Sabbath Economics*. The Church of the Saviour, 2006.

Nouwen, Henri. *Gracias! A Latin American Journal*. Orbis, 2005.

Rutba House, The, editor. *School(s) for Conversion: 12 Marks of a New Monasticism*. Cascade, 2005.

Stock, Jon, Tim Otto, and Jonathan Wilson-Hartgrove. *Inhabiting the Church: Biblical Wisdom for a New Monasticism*. Cascade, 2007.

Wallis, Jim, and Joyce Hollyday, editors. *Cloud of Witnesses*. Orbis, 1994.

Williams, Rowan, *Where God Happens: Discovering Christ in One Another* (New Seeds, 2005.

Wilson-Hartgrove, Jonathan. *To Baghdad and Beyond: How I Got Born Again in Babylon*. Cascade, 2005.

Wright, N. T. *Simply Christian: Why Christianity Makes Sense*. HarperOne, 2006.

Yoder, John Howard. *To Hear the Word*. Wipf and Stock, 1998.

school for conversion
LATIN AMERICA

IMMIGRATING TO THE KINGDOM OF GOD
BORDER CROSSING AND THE MISSION OF THE CHURCH IN THE AMERICAS

Immigrating to the Kingdom of God is an immersion-learning "pilgrimage" experience organized through *School for Conversion—Latin America.** It is designed for small groups who are interested in being immersed into the challenges and possibilities that the church faces in Latin America in order to reenter their own local context by "starting with the nearest neighbor."

Taking the Brazilian context as a "marker" for understanding Christian identity and mission as a global and local reality, the action/reflection components are organized around two **questions** that are as relevant and practical today as they were 25 years ago, when posed by Latin American theologian, Orlando Costas:

(1) "What is it about the Americas that presents a mutual challenge for Christians and their churches?"

(2) "And, further, as followers of Jesus Christ how are we to understand our mission within that reality?"

Objectives:

(1) to give Christians from europe, North America and other economically developed areas the opportunity to have first-hand experience of latin american reality, with its sharp contrasts and contradictions.

(2) to study, analyze and interpret that reality in order to appreciate the challenge that it poses to christian discipleship and mission.

(3) to consider ways in which christians from overseas can work for justice, peace and the integrity of creation in partnership with latin american christians.

Host Cities: São Paulo, Salvador and/or Recife/Olinda.

Dates: To be arranged with local churches/groups.

*For more information about immersion experiences/pilgrimages, see the SFC link and contact info at www.newmonasticism.org/sfc and the blog "On Pilgrimage" at samewell.wordpress.com

Or: Contact Sam Ewell at s_ewell@yahoo.com

EDUCATION *AND* ACTION

School for Conversion is committed to be more than a source of information. We want to be a catalyst for new communities and initiatives that build up the church. So once you've completed this final section of the workbook, please be in touch. Share with us your next step, and let us think and pray with you about how that step leads you closer to God and God's people. We want to connect you with others, come alongside you, and help in any way we can.

You may be in touch via e-mail: info@newmonasticism.org

Or write to:

School for Conversion
917 Berkeley St.
Durham, NC 27705

being w,th
family